The magic trident

Written by Narinder Dhami

Illustrated by Jeffrey Reid

Down, down, down under the sea was a magic kingdom.
The King of the Sea lived there.
He had a magic trident and when he blew on it he could do magic.

One day Nipper the crab asked
the King of the Sea,
'Can you do some magic for me?'
'If you like,' said the king.
'Come with me.'

The king saw a fish. He blew on his magic trident.

Now the fish was red and blue.
'Thank you,' said the fish.

'That's all the magic I'm doing for one day,' said the king, and he went to sleep.

Nipper looked at the magic trident. 'If I had that trident I could do magic too,' he said.

So Nipper ran off with the trident.
'Now I am just like the King of the Sea,' he said.
Just then Nipper saw a fish.
'I will make that fish go red and blue,' he said.

Nipper blew on the magic trident.
But the fish did not go red or blue.
The fish had a green hat on!

'Who put this hat on me?' asked the fish.
'I did,' said Nipper. 'I am not very good at magic.'

Just then Big Mouth the whale swam up.
He looked at the fish in the hat.
'Ha, ha, ha!' laughed Big Mouth.
The fish was cross.
'Get this hat off me,' she said.

Nipper blew on the magic trident.
Now the fish had two hats on!

Big Mouth looked at the fish.
'Ha, ha, ha!' laughed Big Mouth.

Then the fish looked at Big Mouth.
'Ha, ha, ha!' said the fish.
'Now you have a hat on too,' she said.

Big Mouth and the fish were very cross with Nipper.
'Do something!' they said.
'I will go and get the king,' said Nipper.

When the king saw Big Mouth
and the fish he was very cross
with Nipper.
'You must not play with my magic
trident,' he said. 'Give it to me.'

The King of the Sea blew on his magic trident and he made the hats go.
'Thank you,' said Big Mouth and the fish.
'Now what will you do to Nipper?' they asked.

The king looked at Nipper.
Then he blew on his magic trident.

Big Mouth, the fish and the King of the Sea all laughed. Nipper was red and blue and green and pink!